Hearing Voices, Women's Voices

Susan M. King

Presentation by *BookLeaf Publishing*

Web: www.bookleafpub.com

E-mail: info@bookleafpub.com

ISBN: 9789363309067

First edition 2024

*To my daughter, Flora, and my granddaughter,
Willow.*

PREFACE

Yes, I'm hearing voices again. Women's voices.

As both a poet and a preacher, I am always seeking to give voice to the verse that is within me. Sometimes this is a poem, or a sermon, or a song.

May you listen and hear. May your voice be heard.

Hearing Voices

I'm hearing voices again
Women's voices

Strong, soft
Loving, loud
Hurting, hopeful
Quiet, questioning
Challenging, caring
Passionate, protesting
Beguiling, bold

I'm hearing voices again

Chapel

I am that single leaf
In a stained-glass chapel
Hanging for my life
Hanging by a thread

The organ enunciates
Loss and pain
Joy and praise
Prayers murmur like
Whispered confidences

And in my silence I am stretched

Floating

Floating on a perfectly smooth sea
I feel weightless and lifted up
The waves are breaking in the distance
Crashing and foaming
I can see my hands before me
They look small
But very strong

Gratitude

The moon is full and shimmering tonight
So glorious I have to breathe thank you
Thank you as if the magnificent orb
was a private and personal gift just for me
rather than all of humanity
And yet gratitude is necessary for me as air
And so I say thank you

Deeper Than Memory

5

Love

Deeper than memory
Older than words

Hotter than lava
Brighter than sun

Love
Sharper than steel
Vaster than time

Colder than space
Darker than empty

Love

Grandma's Lullaby

6

Sleep, little one, go to sleep
Rest on your pillow your head
Sleep, little one, go to sleep
Now is the time for bed
The world is silent and still
The moon lights the trees on the hill
I love you and I always will
Sleep, little one, go to sleep

My Jewel, My Star

She was so tiny
So much joy wrapped up in one little bundle
My daughter, my jewel
Love for today, hope for tomorrow
Flora

A smile like the sun
Bringing joy to everyone
Laughter that sparkles
She is so tiny
So much joy wrapped up in one little bundle
My granddaughter, my star
Love for today, hope for tomorrow
Willow

Untitled

Post-flood sprinkles
Never materialized into
Expected snow

Instead of snuggling
With her own mom
She lies on poetry

In the whispers of verses
She finds a mother's embrace
A lover's embrace?

Will new life find her?
Will new love revive her?
Beware changes in weather

Friends That Never Fail Us

My grandmother,
Whom I never knew,
Was deaf, and some said, mad.
Books are the "friends that never fail us,"
She wrote as a girl.

Later in life she was abandoned by family and
friends alike.
I find solace in her words
"Books are my best friends, they have never
failed me yet
and I hope they never will."

I hope they never did.

Prayer

Prayer
Whispered or groaned
In hope or desperation
Answered or unanswered

Prayer
At once reaching out and within
Tuning the dial
Making the connection
In hope or desperation

Prayer
They say prayer doesn't change God
Prayer changes you
Let me be changed

Blessing of the Elevator

Bless to me this elevator
carrying people up and down.

Co-workers with healing hearts
and healing hands.

Families anxious for the healing of their
loved ones.

Bless to me this time of waiting,
of anticipation.

Bless the silent companionship
as we travel up and down together
without speaking.

Bless to me each floor and all those
who inhabit it.

Bless to me the opportunity
of each opening of the door.

Bless to me this elevator.

The GIft of Emptiness

The gift of emptiness. Seriously?
How can emptiness possibly be a gift, or bring a
gift?
Isn't emptiness, well, empty?

People fill up their bodies, their time, their
homes
All to keep from feeling empty
That empty feeling that we are not good enough,
not worthy enough, not loveable enough

My faith says Jesus emptied himself for us,
to make space for us
To make space for me

What is taking up space in my heart, in my
mind, in my soul?
Isn't it time to get empty?
Dare I risk emptying myself?
To make room for what cannot be taken, only
received?
To make room for God?
To make room?

A Day Without Stones

It was a day without stones

No massive megaliths towering toward heaven
No carefully heaped cairns signaling sacred
spaces

No water-worn pebbles clattering along brooks
No gravel crunching underfoot

A day without stones

No ammunition for slingshots
No projectiles to smash windows
No sunwarmed roosts among the outcropping
Or cool granite slabs to sit upon

No glittering gemstones
No geode globes bearing shining mystery

No stones to mark graves or keep cars off the
grass
No signposts or guides to keep us on the path
Or mark the lines between life and death

It was a day without stones

Stones 2

Acts 7:54-60, 1 Peter 2:10

That's the funny thing about stones.
Like most inanimate objects, they are morally
neutral.
Good or bad, not in and of themselves
Only depending on how we use them
use for decoration
use for building
use for throwing at each other

Images of stones
Jesus as the cornerstone
Faith as the foundation
you and I as stones
being put together
to build something new
a holy temple
to honor God

Think of the stones we throw
insults, condemnation, putting someone down,
calling someone a demeaning name

Stones of

Religion
Political Ideology
National Origin
Ethnicity/race
Gender
Immigration status

Will we use these differences
as ways to build color and contrast into our
temple
as spice for our stew (not melting pot)
as diversity to cherish
as building blocks
or as stones to attack each other

How will you use your stone?
To throw at someone, to hurt or injure them
To build up our nation, to build up Christ's
church, to build up God's kingdom
You can't do both.

Into Deep Water

Luke 5:1-11

In the town of Magdala,
The home of the one called Mary the
Magdalene,
Can be found the chapel called Duc In Altum --
Latin for "into the deep water."
It is tempting to stay close to shore, paddling
around in the shallows.
But Jesus beckons us into the deep water.

God is calling us out of the shallows into the
deep waters.
Into the deep waters of spirituality,
into the deep waters of compassion and justice
and abundance for all.

Out of the shallows. Into the deep water.
But not alone. And not for ourselves alone.
May it be so.

Mary's Journey to Love

The first step on my journey to love was the
angel.
Oh, you know the story.
Angel. Message from God. Unwed mother.

The next step on my journey did not feel like
love at all.
As difficult as my parents' reactions had been,
it was much harder to take Joseph's.
Disappointed, distressed. Yet he stood by me.

Instead of feeling like love was just beginning,
instead, it felt like love, the love between Joseph
and I, was dying.

My journey of love took me to Bethlehem.
To a crowded, busy city where there was no
room for a young mother-to-be. Where there was
no room for a miracle.
It took me to a stable.

And it took me to a cross.
The foot of a cross where my son was brutally
executed.

Where was love then?
It was only later that I understood how the cross
was God's love
shining out to the world.
As much as a star that showed the way.
As much as an angels' chorus.
As much as a stable bed for a tiny baby.

I don't know where your journey to love begins.
I don't know what path it will take.
I don't know what joys and what sorrows will be
revealed on the way.
But I do know that it will lead you to a stable.
I know it will lead you to a cross.
I know it will lead you to an empty tomb.
And I know your journey will begin and end
with love.

The love of God that shown so brightly so many
years ago.
The love of God reflected in the love others
show to you,
and the love of God that you show to others.

The Bride

John 2:1-11

I have a bone to pick. After all, it was MY
wedding.
My wedding and I was not even mentioned in
the story.

As it turned out, the celebration almost ended in
disaster.
For the worst possible thing imaginable
happened. The wine ran out.

What's a wedding feast without wine?
Not just because wine is often the only safe
thing to drink.
But wine is a sign of celebration, of abundance,
of joy.
We use wine for trade, we use wine in worship,
we use wine to mark special occasions.
What's a wedding feast without wine?

It's a good thing that I wasn't aware what was
happening at the time.
I would have been devastated and embarrassed
in front of all those people,

that the wine had run out.

I only learned later that Jesus had instructed the
servants to fill empty jars with water,
and when they drew it out, it was wine!

Not any old jars, either, but the stone water jars
for the rites of purification, each holding twenty
or thirty gallons. Six stone jars when one would
have been more than enough!

Not any old wine, but the best wine people had
ever tasted!

The miracle of the wine at the wedding, my
wedding,
became known as a sign; a sign of God's
presence with Jesus in a powerful way;
a sign of God's power and love revealed in our
everyday life.

All of us have times when like it feels like the
wine has run out.
Times when it feels like all the joy and hope in
our lives has dried up
and all that is left is a hollow, empty jar.

In those times, remember the day when the wine
ran out.

And remember that is not how the story ended.
Remember that God saved the best for last.

21

A Little Oil

2 Kings 4:1-7

She was a widow with children dependent upon
her
Creditors were knocking at the door, ready to
take her children as slaves.
She had nothing left but a little oil.

What good is a little oil? How could she protect
her children?
Nothing but a little oil. So little in the face of
such a calamity.
She had lost her protector and didn't know
where to turn.

So she turned to the great prophet Elisha.
Surely he could perform a miracle for her.
Only a miracle could help them now.
A miracle, not just a little bit of oil.

Elisha asked her what she had. Just a little bit of
oil
And told her to gather all the containers she
could find
And pour the oil into them.

It didn't make sense. God's instructions are often
this way.
So she gathered bottles and jars and cups and
pots and began pouring.
And pouring and pouring. She kept pouring out
that little bit of oil
Until she had nowhere else to pour it.

A quiet miracle. The oil flowed and flowed to
overflowing.
Sell all that oil, the prophet told her.
Sell all that oil and buy your children back.
A quiet miracle. Flowing and overflowing.
Like God's love, flowing and overflowing.

The children were saved.
Yet many children are in danger even now.
Do you have a little oil?

Rahab

Joshua Chapter 2

The world's oldest profession.
That's what they euphemistically call it.
I call it my only way to survive.

Without a husband to protect me.
Without education or skills.
How else was I supposed to provide for myself
and for those who were depending upon me?

It all started with a couple of enemy spies.
Why I let them into my house in the first place I
can't explain.

Then the King of Jericho himself sent a
messenger
asking for their whereabouts.
And I lied. That's what I'm remembered for.
I lied to my own king.

Truth was, I had hidden those spies under stalks
of flax
I told the king's men I didn't know where they
had come from

or where they were going

For I had heard of their god, the God of Israel.
I knew that they were going to prevail over the
city of Jericho.
And so I begged for my family's safety, for them
to be spared.

"Our lives for your lives!" the spies promised.
Put a scarlet cord in your window and your
family will be saved.
Could they (and their God) be trusted?

And so it was.
Jericho was defeated. My family was spared.
I married a man of the Hebrew people
and gave birth to a son named Boaz.

Boaz married another foreign woman,
whose name was Ruth.
She gave birth to Obed, who was the father of
Jesse,
and Jesse the father of King David.

Are you shocked that the family tree of Jesus
goes back to a lying prostitute?
All I can say is that God often works through
the most unlikely of people.

And I beg of you,
do not let my story
fuel your claim that God takes sides in human
wars.

It's a story about faith
not a justification for war.
May it be so.

Home in the Islands

Back in Hawaii where it feels like home
Though I lived here for a dozen years, it is not
my home
Nor will it ever truly be
I was not born and raised here,
not truly a child of the land, the 'aina

Not a tourist,
I consider myself a returning guest
Welcomed back with aloha by both people and
'aina
Never to be taken for granted

There are some who would see me as an intruder
A symbol of those who overthrew the monarchy
Who suppressed language and culture
Who took over the land

Still Hawaii calls to me
The beauty of the ocean, the waterfalls, the cliffs
and the sunsets
The grace of the hula and the lilting strains of
Hawaiian music

I long to return but I can never stay

Too expensive to live here
Too far from my family

But even if I could stay,
I would never want to displace
A child of the 'aina who is forced
Into exile on the Mainland, like so many

Here for a brief respite
In the tension between
The sins of the past
The inequities of the present
And the anxieties of the future

Tradewinds blow
And it still feels like home